MW00830042

Other books by
Erik Kanto & Ilona Kanto:

Faces Tell

How to Conquer Hollywood

NOTICE ABOUT THIS BOOK'S PHOTO IMAGES:
In this book, the photos, as well as the face readings
attached to those photos, do not represent the face
readings of the persons in those photos. The images are
used only as examples of the facial features described
in the content of the book.

Cover: Kate Nyberg, photo by Erik Kanto.
Cover design by Leena Hannonen.

Your Face Tells All

Learn the Wisdom of the Chinese Art of Face Reading

Erik Kanto & Ilona Kanto

Published by Atophill Publishing
P.O. Box 630435, Simi Valley, CA 93063, USA.
www.atophill.com

Copyright ©MMIV by Kanto Productions LLC
and Atophill Publishing.
Printed in the United States of America.

Photos: *Liberace* courtesy of Dora Liberace, The Liberace Foundation for the Performing and Creative Arts; *Uma Thurman & Erik Kanto* by HFPA; *Ronn Moss, Debbie Allen* by Ilona Kanto, all others by Erik Kanto.
Graphic illustrations: Ilona Kanto

Face reading experts: Peter Shen, Ilona Kanto, Erik Kanto

First Edition
ISBN 1-929956-13-4
Library of Congress Control Number 2004090351

Kanto, Erik
   Your face tells all : learn the wisdom of the Chinese
art of face reading / Erik Kanto & Ilona Kanto
   p. cm.
   Includes index.
   ISBN 1-929956-13-4

   1. Physiognomy.   I. Kanto, Ilona   II. Title.

BF851.K36 2004   138
                         QBI04-200026

Your Face Tells All

Overview

Who is the best mate for me? Will I be rich? Will I have a long healthy life? A happy marriage? Do I have the potential to become a famous actor or a Nobel Prize-winning scientist? These are questions we all have in mind. The wisdom of Chinese face reading may give us the answers, and they are written all over our face.

The ancient Chinese art of face reading was first developed more than 2,500 years ago and, in one form or another, Physiognomy, or the art of discovering inner character and quality from outward appearance, has fascinated people all over the world ever since. By looking at a person's face and its features, the reader gets a lot of information: the temperament, potential, disposition, creativity, and whether the person is, or will be, fortunate or not so fortunate.

In face reading, the features and other facial characteristics show personality qualities and internal gifts as well as sex life, popularity and life expectancy; however, in their wisdom, the Chinese do not consider any feature as strictly bad or good.

If something is unfortunate, we may ask what compensates that feature, and, as a result, what good will become of that. If another feature is good, we should ask what it is good for. It is important for you to know your own assets and vulnerabilities. For instance, the ears represent life possibilities. A person with small ears may not be capable of holding onto his or her success, but then again, that person is often artistic with good taste and good manners. And even though a large-eared person sometimes has a tendency to get into accidents, he or she has large ideas and sees matters as a whole.

This book reveals all the basics of this mysterious Chinese art. It presents photos of well-known Hollywood celebrities as examples of face types and features, making study easy and fascinating. When people learn to understand their own personality, it helps them to guide their choice of careers and to get along with other people. And, studying and interpreting faces brings the face reader greater appreciation of others.

Your face provides the answers to your most important questions about compatibility with a potential life partner, prospects for success in business, and creates a successful life plan. Face reading provides valuable knowledge that can help us make the right decisions about the people we meet and deal with, and it can give us insight into ourselves.

Introduction

My first experience with Physiognomy, or face reading, happened in a peculiar way. I was flying from New York to Los Angeles when next to me sat a man with Chinese features. His name was Peter Shen. The flight had been overbooked, and the airplane was completely full. Peter Shen had missed an earlier flight after being stuck in traffic. Still, for some reason, even when not a single seat was available and several passengers with confirmed seats were left at the airport, there he was, on the same flight with me.

We started talking quite normally, chatting about congested airports and the service in airplanes. Then the topic shifted toward the interests of both parties: entertainment business, television and movie productions. I found out that Shanghai-born Peter Shen was not only well known in theatre, film and television productions and the makeup industry, but he was also a respected and skilled expert in Chinese face reading. His lectures and books had been great successes around the world.

After hours of flying and the most intriguing discussions, I reached an agreement with Shen to create and produce Chinese face reading topics for television, print and multimedia projects.

This was the start of a fascinating era in my and my wife Ilona's lives. For years, a lot with Peter's expertise, we studied the secrets of Physiognomy. The deeper we went the more interesting and spellbinding it became. Because our work in Hollywood entails daily dealings with famous celebrities, we have a large personal collection of their photographs. So in addition to studying the rules of face reading, we were able to interpret hundreds of celebrity faces.

A skeptic might say that it is extremely easy for anyone to read the face of a celebrity, since everyone knows what she or he is like. But, for the book of face reading in the Finnish language, published in Finland, we asked Peter to read also several Finnish celebrities' faces and their facial characteristics that he most certainly had never seen before. To our great amazement, by reading their 8" x 10" photos, Peter described these people and their lives as if he had always known them. The only Finnish person he knew beforehand was the 1952 Miss Universe, Finland's own Armi Kuusela.

When reading this book, you should have a mirror close by. You will see yourself in a totally new light, and I promise that by the last page, you will have learned many new things about your family members, friends and colleagues. Remember also to read the photo captions, and sometimes it helps to read between the lines...

The Chinese have seriously studied Physiognomy for thousands of years. The Western world still considers it as a form of entertainment, but a form of entertainment that can reveal great secrets from our past, present and future. But don't run and schedule cosmetic surgery to change your fortune. As the studies reveal, it is not the way to change something that has already been planned for you; however, once you know your future, you can change it merely by living a different life, perhaps by becoming a new person or changing the way you live or think.

During one of my lectures on face reading—this was far away from Hollywood—when using the facial characteristics of Hollywood celebrity John Goodman's photo— an elderly man from the audience raised the question, "Why are you showing the photo of this man on the screen? I've no idea who he is." Before I had time to answer, another person from the audience replied: "I know him! He's Bob! Bob Stevenson from Dead wood, South Dakota. I know him!" And after that we discussed the features on the face of Bob Stevenson from Deadwood, South Dakota. That is the point: study the features of the celebrity faces, and the stories that they tell you. It does not matter if you do not recognize those photos. They are familiar to many, but then again, even if you do not know them, you can find there the facial characteristics that your uncle, or mother, or spouse, or anyone you know has.

Perhaps one of the reasons for the creation of this book is to help us to understand why people look different from each other, and why those differences make them unique. I also believe that this book will answer many questions we all have as to why certain things in life work and others do not. Why our relationships sometimes succeed, and sometimes don't. Why it appears that for some people, situations easily resolve themselves, and for others they cause a lot of pain.

One more thing: For thousands of years the Chinese have believed that lengthy laugh lines on your mouth predict a long life, and the ability to see many generations to come. So, when we meet, let's smile!

Erik Kanto
Hollywood, California

Thanks

We would like to thank all those people whose facial features—published on these pages or not—helped create this book. Also, a great many thanks to our Chinese face reading expert Peter Shen, now our friend, who most likely saw promising features on our faces. Of course, our special thanks to our parents, Edit and Toivo Särkkä, and Sirkka and Matti Kanto, as well as our grandparents and great grandparents, whose genes and life-lines helped us grow to where we are now.

Our copy editor and friend Jack Tewksbury who did an excellent job, and Leena Hannonen, Macnetic Design, for pre-press consultation; thank you.

Erik Kanto & Ilona Kanto

TABLE OF CONTENTS

CHAPTER FOUR: SEVEN OTHER FEATURES

CHAPTER FIVE: OTHER FACIAL FEATURES

CHAPTER SIX: CLOSING

INDEX   170

CHAPTER ONE:
WHAT YOUR FACE CAN TELL

An Ideal Face
The Three Zones

AN IDEAL FACE

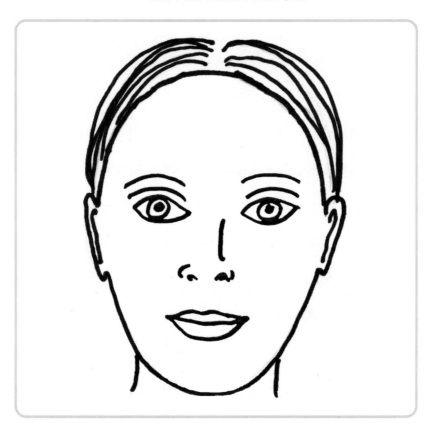

When describing the ideal face, the Chinese do not specify a face with oriental features, but a face with very universal characteristics. According to Physiognomy, three horizontal parts, zones, of the face—the forehead, the middle section and the lower part—should ideally be of equal height. The eyebrows should be even and curved, and the area between the eyes should be two-fingers broad. The nose should be straight and well-shaped. The most important aspect for an ideal face is that all the features are balanced when compared to each other.

Halle Berry

A beautiful face: Everything is perfectly balanced. All three zones are of equal length. This is a Gold face with luminous eyes, and the whole look is very elegant. Often Gold people marry another Gold person because they associate in similar social surroundings. Gold does better, however, with the solid Earth, who provides the needed strength that Earth can give.

THE THREE ZONES

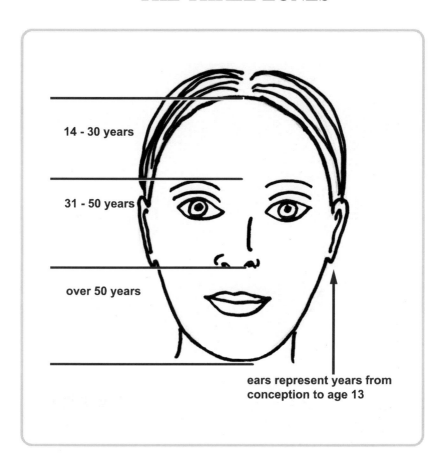

14 - 30 years

31 - 50 years

over 50 years

ears represent years from
conception to age 13

The face is divided into three zones. These zones reveal a person's past, present and future. The ears represent childhood, from conception to age 13. The left ear, starting from the top, reveals the years before birth to 6, and the right ear shows the years 7-13. The top part of the face, from the hairline to the eyebrows, represents youth, age 14 through 30. The information it gives includes intelligence and memory. The area from the eyebrows to the bottom of the nose represents mid-life, age 31-50. It reveals the person's relationship to money and emotions. The lower part of the face, from the bottom of the nose to the tip of the chin, represents maturity, age fifty and after.

If the zones are balanced—all three parts are of equal height—it indicates a balanced, productive life. Content childhood and upbringing is—or was—followed by excellent results in mid-life, and all those lead up to a comfortable old age. If one zone is dominant, it indicates the part of life in which the individual will be most effective. For instance, if the top zone is clearly dominant, that person remains youthful and he or she achieves the most before the thirtieth birthday. When the middle zone is stronger than the others, it is very important for that person to accomplish many things during his or her life. And, of course, the best achievements are reached in mid-life. Further on, if the bottom zone of the face is significantly stronger than the others, we have a familyperson, whose life is at its best during his or her later years.

The shortest zone indicates the part of life in which you may have most of your problems. Those can be health, wealth, relationship or emotional challenges. A short top zone indicates problems in youth or at school. A short middle zone suggests difficulties in finding the right place and position in life. And a short bottom zone warns that the person should pay special attention to his or her health in the years after the age of fifty. It may also reflect money problems or solitude in old age.

We should remember that these zones reflect their energy from one to another. Thus, a very dominant forehead does not mean that life is over at thirty; on the contrary, the energy achieved in youth may carry through to—and sometimes challenging—the middle years. Likewise, a strong middle zone may help to ease struggles in old age.

Even ugly faces are worth looking at—and that is a great comfort for most people.

Chinese proverb.

Tom Cruise

*The middle zone of the face is strong, so in the middle part
of his life he does better than in the early part of his life.
The non-existing earlobes indicate there may have been
problems during childhood and he was not well taken care
of. But the nose is very strong; especially the bridge
of the nose, which is very prominent.*

CHAPTER TWO:
THE FACE SHAPES

The Theory of Five Elements
Glamorous Gold
The Intriguing Fire People
Wealthy Water
Secure Earth
The Far-Sighted Wood People
The Combinations
Yin and Yang

THE THEORY OF FIVE ELEMENTS

The first aspect we should pay attention to is the shape of the face. There are five elements: Fire, Water, Earth, Gold, and Wood, and each one is associated with a particular face shape. The ancient Chinese watched the sky and knew five planets: Mars, Mercury, Saturn, Venus and Jupiter. In China, each planet was associated with the particular element for which it was named. Mars—Fire Star, Mercury—Water Star, Saturn—Earth Star, Venus—Gold Star and Jupiter—Wood Star.

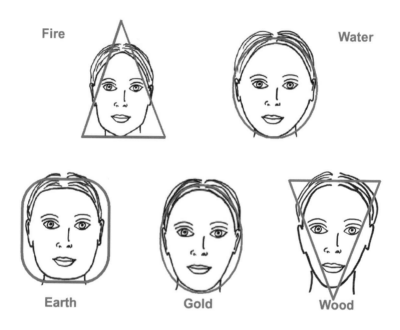

There are also three common face shapes that are combinations of two elements: Gold and Wood, Water and Wood, Fire and Wood; however, any elemental face type may combine with any other element, and in combinations, elements may help or hinder one another.

What you can learn right away about yourself or someone else from the elements is the easiest part of face reading: All pure types are effective people. All mixed types are either positive or stressful, depending on the beneficial or detracting effect of the combined elements and the degree to which the weakening element is present. And in choosing a partner, it is wise not to choose someone of your own element.

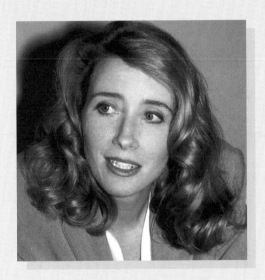

Emma Thompson

This is a very good face with an excellent composition and a lot of balance and harmony. Every feature fits in a correct place. The oblong-shaped face belongs to the Gold element. Balanced features like these help the owner to achieve a very high status in society. The nose is interesting, as it is straight with a pointed tip, which shows this person is very much a perfectionist. The lips curve up so she is a very positive person.

GLAMOROUS GOLD

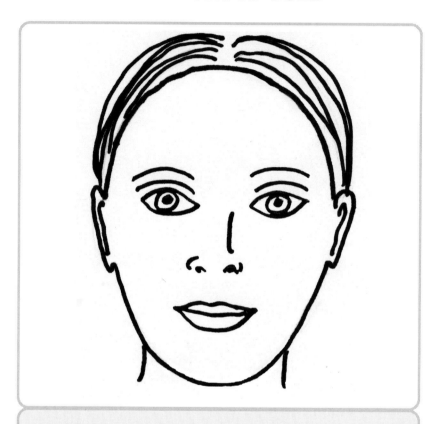

Element: Gold
Planet: Venus
Color: White
Facial Shape: Oblong
Skin Type: Dewy
Overall Feature: Elegant
Helping Element: Earth helps Gold—supporting Gold's vanity
Hindering Element: Fire hinders Gold—as we know fire
can melt gold
Health: Pay special attention to lungs

Gold represents the beautiful planet Venus, which in most cultures is a symbol of beauty and delight. The Chinese consider this oblong face the perfect balance in face shapes, and you can see the same proportions on the ancient Greek statues. Each zone of the face is equal in length and width, compared to each other. The genuine Gold personality is easy to spot in a crowd with the person's radiant eyes, perfect face shape, softly rounded ears, and the posture of royalty. Gold people have enough grace and charm to give to everyone, but often they just keep everything to themselves.

It seems that anything a Gold person does will be a huge success and that makes him or her a definite image-maker. Very often they have a high social standing and enjoy the limelight. Many actors, models and leaders are more or less of the Gold element; however, you should not envy them too much—all the outside perfection does not mean that Gold people are ideal. Frequently they lack inner strength, and because of their vanity they team up with people like themselves. In Hollywood, you very rarely see a long-lasting marriage between two Gold persons.

THE INTRIGUING FIRE PEOPLE

Element: Fire
Planet: Mars
Color: Red
Facial Shape: Conic
Skin Type: Reddish
Overall Feature: Sharp pointed
Helping Element: Wood helps Fire—with Wood's intelligence
Hindering Element: Water hinders Fire—by turning Fire's energy down
Health: You should take good care of your heart

Like the flame of a candle, the face of a Fire element is broad around the jaw and narrows towards the top of the head. In real life, fire is restless, frequently changing its form, and that is also the nature of a Fire person. People with the pure element also have bony fingers and sharp, visible cheekbones. Their hair is often curly and usually of a bright color.

You will never have a dull moment with Fire personalities. They are exciting, unpredictable, gregarious and impatient. They love making new friends and it is very easy to start a conversation with them. If you are not very talkative, they always have things to chatter about. A Fire person does not make a good team with Gold, as the grace of Gold tends to melt under Fire's endless actions. A much better companion might be a Wood person, who can provide the wisdom Fire often lacks.

*Your face, my thane, is a book
where men may read strange matters.*

William Shakespeare, Macbeth.

Ronn Moss

*This is a Fire face because the jaw line is very prominent.
The lips are full and they belong to a passionate person. But
when persons such as this have jaw lines strong and broad,
they can be self-centered. They worry about themselves and
do not much care about the other people around them.*

WEALTHY WATER

Element: Water
Planet: Mercury
Color: Black
Facial Shape: Round
Skin Type: Moist
Overall Feature: Round
Helping Element: Gold helps Water—Gold's status and Water's money go well together
Hindering Element: Earth hinders Water—by blocking the circulation of Water
Health: Pay attention to your kidneys

A typical Water face is round, without any visible bone structure. As with water, a Water person's hands are often round and soft. Generous sweating is one of the features of this element, as are mobile lips and often protruding eyes.

Just as water behaves in nature, the Water personality very easily settles into new situations. As a rule, Water people easily accumulate wealth, and are good at business. They are clear-headed, able to benefit from the most demanding business negotiations, and their way of thinking is bright and witty. Due to their sharp minds, Water people are excellent in diplomatic careers. Their fleshy face hides all the facial bones, including facial expressions, and that gives them extra vigor in diplomatic or business negotiations, as well as sitting at a poker table.

For marriage, Gold is the perfect choice for Water. The Water person might lack the grace and beauty of Gold, but a Gold person's social status enhances the Water person's ability to make even more money.

Rob Reiner

This face carries a lot of Water, so clearly the person is capable of making a lot of money. The ears are large so he is well-protected and has a long life. The nose is strong which shows that in the middle years, he will do anything he wants and will accomplish his goals.

Better a bald head than no head at all.

Seumas MacManus

SECURE EARTH

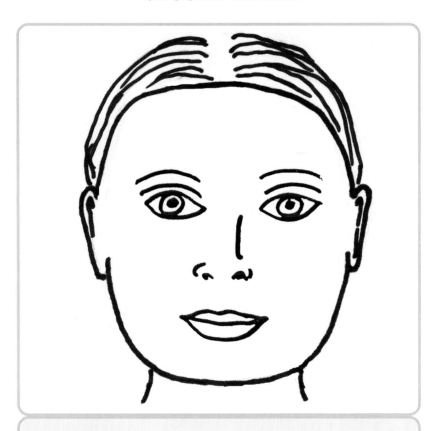

Element: Earth
Planet: Saturn
Color: Yellowish brown
Facial Shape: Square
Skin Type: Firm
Overall Feature: Bulky
Helping Element: Fire helps Earth—by bringing Earth to life
Hindering Element: Wood hinders Earth—their philosophy
is millions of miles apart
Health: The stomach is your weakest area.

A square face is a key to the Earth element, which is the most stable of the five elements. An Earth person has wide jaw line and approximately the same width forehead. The chin and lips are thick and the ears are large. Overall, everything is large and well-balanced. The Earth person is forceful, an achiever. He or she can be stubborn, but then again, the Earth person's word is the same as a written contract. Individuals with the Earth element try to find a permanent, secure home, and once it has been found, that is the fortress they defend with all their capabilities.

Earth people often pair up with the same element, but then life can be boringly steady and secure. That is why a Fire person can be a much more refreshing companion than most.

*A person without a smiling face
must never open a shop.*

Chinese proverb.

Michael Douglas

This is a combination of Wood and Earth. Even though it is a very aspiring and intelligent face, there seem to be a lot of hidden conflicts here. No matter how much he accomplishes, he still feels the need to do more. The eyebrows are nicely arched. The eyes are dreamy, indicating many dreams and great visions, and that whatever he is doing now will not be good enough. He feels compelled to always do more, and to work harder. The nose is interesting, and the flare of the nostrils shows he has a lot of passion.

He is a very emotional person.

THE FAR-SIGHTED WOOD PEOPLE

Element: Wood
Planet: Jupiter
Color: Green
Facial Shape: Triangle
Skin Type: Compact
Overall Feature: Lengthy
Helping Element: Water helps Wood—often financially
Hindering Element: Gold hinders Wood—Gold easily
looks down on Wood
Health: Pay attention to your liver.

Again, as in nature, wood, in the form of a tree, is typically narrow on the bottom, becoming wider the higher we look. Thus the Wood face is of a triangle shape, narrower at the bottom and wider at the top. Other typical features are a high forehead and long ears and nose. Of the five elements, Wood is the most spiritual and honest. The same way you can trust the word of an Earth person, you can take the Wood's word to the bank. In addition, like a tree, the Wood person has the ability to see farther and in a much broader span than other people. Their greatest yearning is to solve the secrets of the universe, and they spend a lot of time planning and dreaming about something that they eventually never are able to materialize.

Most likely a Wood person marries another Wood type, and they can have a great time together. However, after a while, they fall down from the clouds and realize that one of them should start doing the everyday tasks such as house cleaning and grocery shopping. As mentioned earlier, Fire is a much better selection, unless the Wood person finds him or her too frivolous.

Robin Williams

This is a typical Wood face: Inspiring, creative, sensitive. The face of a poet! And with those very fortunate ears, he is an exceptionally kind-hearted person. The eyes are mischievous, so he likes to have fun and likes to create a lot of joy around him. The mouth has a very thin upper lip and a thick lower lip, showing he has the savvy to be a lawyer.

THE COMBINATIONS

Very rarely a person will have the facial features of only one element. That is why we also have to study combinations of elements. The three most common combinations are Gold & Wood, Water & Wood and Fire & Wood. In addition, the features of any element or any combination may carry individual features from any other element(s). In combination those features may either help or hinder other existing features.

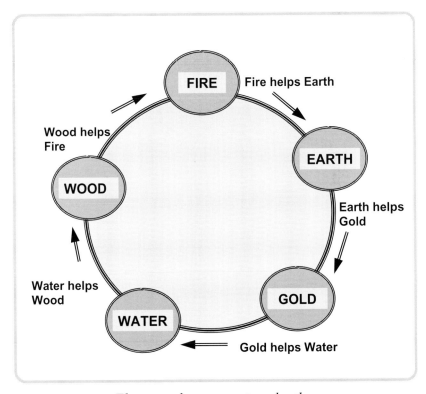

Elements that support each other

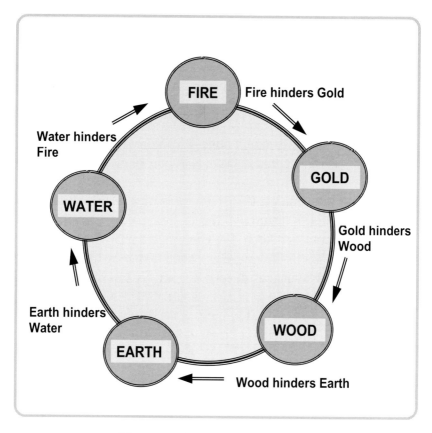

Elements that hinder each other

When studying these circles, we should bear in mind that they illustrate symbolic names for energies, or elements, and the relationships between those energies. Five energies evolve their natural way, one after the other in a supportive cycle. This is called the Supportive Order of Five Elements. In the circle of elements that hinder each other, these five energies slow down or stop the development of the strength and influence of the corresponding elements.

Fire hinders Gold because fire melts metal. The energy of Fire that flares up and heats stops the smooth and flexible movement of Gold from condensing and solidifying. If Fire is weak, Gold becomes stiff and it loses its structure. If Fire is too strong, Gold is not able to concentrate its inner energy and it will lose its appearance.

Gold hinders Wood. If Gold is weak, Wood's interference is too strong. If Gold is dominating, it can damage Wood.

Wood hinders Earth because wood draws nutrients from earth. Earth's moving energy is stopped or slowed down by Wood's expanding growth energy. If Wood is weak, Earth is also powerless. If Wood is strong, it disturbs Earth.

Earth hinders Water. The energy of Earth that tends to go around limits Water's energy, which has a tendency to fall down. If Earth is weak, Water goes deeper. If Earth is too strong, it holds back, as with a dam, the natural movement of Water.

Water hinders Fire. The upwards-flowing energy of Fire can be balanced by Water that is flowing downwards. If the energy of Water is weak, too much Fire could evaporate Water. If Water is too strong, it can suffocate Fire.

For example, a face with a strong Fire element, whose skin usually is reddish, is helped by the grayish-greenish tone that is created by Wood. Then again, the Water element weakens Fire and that can be recognized from a darkish tone of the face; however, only a small portion of the Gold element—the light tones—won't weaken Wood if the person is otherwise strong.

The first thing we can learn about a person almost immediately, is that if one element is very clear and no other elements are hindering, and if the color tones of the skin are correct, that person is a strong individual. People with combinations of elements on their faces are either very positive or very frustrated, depending on the combining energy's hindering or helping and on how visible that energy is on the face.

Jamie Lee Curtis

Here is a typical Wood face. She has a lot of excellent ideas and she is very creative. The eyes are deep, which reveals that she is very alert. The mouth is wide, which brings to light a lot of pleasant frames of mind.

When we study our own elements, we can also learn if another person's elements are hindering or helping us. When selecting a partner for life or work, it is not a good idea to choose someone whose dominant element is the same as your own. A much better idea is to choose someone with facial elements that help and support your own facial elements and energies. That way we can help and support not only ourselves, but those close to us as well.

Clint Eastwood

This is a very interesting face. A typical triangle shape belongs to the Wood element. This person is aspiring, creative, and the eyes are much focused. He has a lot of intensive energy, and he does not tolerate any kind of disturbance in his life. When this person wants something, he will get it—on his terms. Ears are very tight, which shows that he does not worry what the others want.

YIN AND YANG

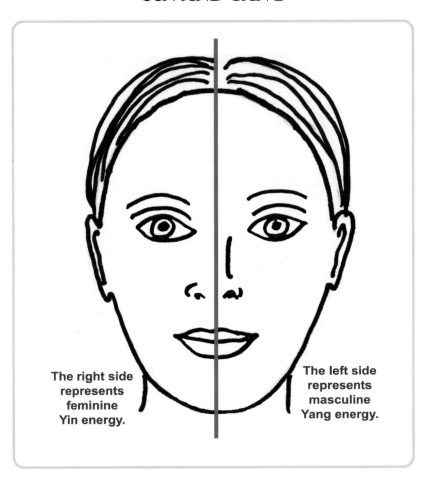

The right side represents feminine Yin energy.

The left side represents masculine Yang energy.

Yin and Yang energies in the Chinese Face Reading.

To study a face, we should always look at the face as whole. According to Chinese studies, the Chi energy that flows throughout the world is combined from two entities opposite to each other, Yin and Yang, which also complement and balance each other. Yin represents feminine energy: Night, darkness, moisture and quiet. Yang represents masculine energy: Bright, day, dry and filled with sound. One side and the qualities it presents may be dominating, but both Yin and Yang are present everywhere. Yin and Yang energies attract each other so that a person with strong Yin can be incredibly attracted to a person that has strong Yang.

When we vertically divide the face into two equal sections, the left side represents masculine Yang energy. It reveals if that person is aggressive, logical, assertive, focused and captivating. It also discloses the fathers' and grandfathers' influences on that person. If Yang is the stronger energy of the two, that person often has thin lips and a forceful chin.

The Yin energy on the right side of the face represents flexibility, creativity, and passion and it shows the influences of the feminine ancestry. The studies indicate the Yin side is able to show a great variety of emotions and feelings, whereas the Yang side hides any passion or feeling. If Yin is dominating on the face, the person very often has large eyes and a hefty nose.

If Cleopatra's nose had been flat, the face of the world would have been changed.

Brander Matthews

CHAPTER THREE:
FIVE MOST IMPORTANT FEATURES

The Ears
The Eyebrows
The Eyes
The Nose
The Mouth

The five most important features of your face are ears, eyebrows, eyes, nose and mouth. They tell about a person's possibilities to advance in life.

FEATURES	AFFECT TO
EARS	LIFE'S POTENTIAL
EYEBROWS	REPUTATION
EYES	WISDOM
NOSE	WEALTH, MID-LIFE ACHIEVEMENTS
MOUTH	DISPOSITION

Five most important features and where they affect.

Mena Suvari

These eyes are very interesting. They show one who is naturally outgoing, sensitive and artistic. Large-eyed people succeed in the theatre and other arts. Women with these kinds of eyes do not make good homemakers, because they want to be out sharing a broader experience.

THE EARS

The ears show a person's abilities and life possibilities. Their basic shape resembles that of a fetus in a womb, and according to Chinese studies the overall shape, size and position reveal how

the baby was nourished and treated in his or her nursing period and early childhood. The good qualities are a large size, an even shape, long earlobes, and a position close to the head. The tops of the ears should be at least high enough to reach the outside level of the eye corners. Unusual features in the ear, including ears that stick out, may bring childhood problems to light.

A large ear with a long earlobe.

An interesting detail of ears is that in general, they do not change their overall shape when the child grows into adulthood. A child with a puffy outer edge of the ear is often given too much attention as a child and he or she may become very selfish as an adult. Also, an overactive child with thin, sharp-edged ears and very little earlobe may grow up to be a rather irresponsible adult. We really should also pay attention to the color tones of the ears. Normally they should be of a lighter tone than the face, with the earlobe slightly reddish. Ears that are constantly red reveal an inconsiderate mind and short temper. Ears darker than the facial coloring often tell of the lack of life's energies. That person is hardly ever interested in spiritual growth, only in gathering money and property.

As mentioned earlier, sizable ears give away a positive image, and if they also have long earlobes, they indicate intelligence, willingness to try, and pleasant years throughout life. Small ears are often located in the middle zone of the head, which portrays the best achievements during the ages between thirty-one and fifty. People with small ears usually have excellent manners and they love colors and music.

If you love being impulsive and having fun, and don't take life too seriously, check to see if your earlobes are narrow. Unfortunately you may also be known for not keeping your word, especially in a relationship.

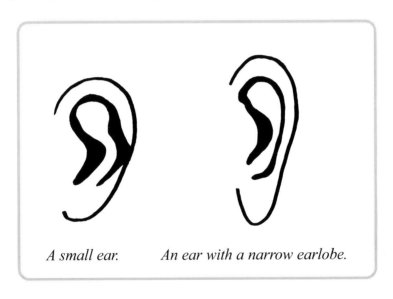

A small ear.   *An ear with a narrow earlobe.*

How high the ears are positioned on the sides of the head has an extensive result. Ears so high that the tops reach above the eyebrows suggest abilities and remarkable intelligence early in life, because the top part of the ear is in the top zone, the youth area. If those ears are also very long, with the lobes reaching all the way to the lowest horizontal zone, the youth's energy will carry on past long the fiftieth birthday.

Most successful people in the world often have ears located wholly in the middle zone. Their best years are in middle age, and—of course—the ears that extend down to the bottom zone of the face guarantee success for years to come.

Ears that are high.

If the top of the ear is lower than the eyes, it implies that the person is living a rather careless life. Why bother to work up a sweat when someone else can do it! If a husband has ears like that, he usually enjoys seeing his wife working, while he is out having fun. If the wife's ears are very low, she most likely doesn't love work either at home or out, but prefers living on her husband's salary. In general, and this applies to friendships and working partners as well, a person like that is rarely interested in contributing to any kind of joint income or effort. On the other hand, if those low ears continue all the way into the lower zone of the face, there is a good likelihood that new opportunities and willingness to work for them will show up in later years, even long after fifty.

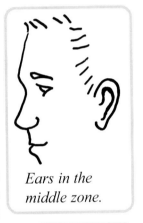

Ears in the middle zone.

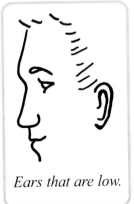

Ears that are low.

Debbie Allen

This is a typical oval-shaped face, with a combination of Gold and Wood. The ears are surprisingly high, meaning she can achieve a lot before the middle years. She has a very round forehead and that shows she is a very intelligent person. The nose is strong, and the mouth is extensive, so she is passionate but very strong-minded at the same time. The left eye is larger than the right one, which can mean that the person may become aggressive.

Steven Spielberg

This face belongs to the Wood element. He is very creative, artistic, aspiring. Large ears indicate a person who has large ideas and sees matters as a whole. If the person in this photo weren't in show business, he would be a scientist, or a creator.

THE EYEBROWS

The eyebrows tell about person's fame and reputation. If somebody wants to become famous in motion pictures, theatre, arts, or politics, it is important that the eyebrows are strong and visible. The eyebrows reveal how other people see us, and they express the person's temperament and ability to engage in relationships.

Ideal eyebrows.

Ideal eyebrows are long and elegant, they have an even curve, and they are slightly thicker at the ends in the center of the face. The inner and outer end should be horizontally on the same level. Ideally the distance between the brows is the width of two fingers.

Strongly curved eyebrows.

Strongly curved eyebrows illustrate a superior reputation. You may see them on the faces of people who have achieved great success in their lives, or who can, when they so desire, easily accomplish their goals. That person is mentally well balanced and very harmonious in relationships, with a sincere, artistic and romantic nature.

Eyebrows that curve upward.

Eyebrows that curve upward reveal a person that is very active. Words such as positive, aggressive, proud, sexy, determined, hardworking and full of self-esteem are excellent descriptions. This person wants to stretch his or her energy out everywhere, and there is a strong potentiality for directorial jobs. If those eyebrows are also soft and evenly formed, the person is likely to achieve fame and glory. If they instead are uneven and weedy, that may demonstrate dictatorial qualities in that person.

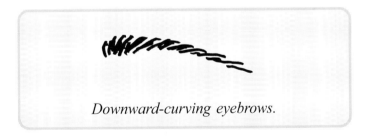

Downward-curving eyebrows.

Downward-curving eyebrows tell that their owner is submissive and always complaining, never satisfied with what he or she has. People around that person tend to think he or she was born to be a loser. However, this individual's strength is very much based on that. When people only believe in this person's weaknesses, they want to give help and support. And this personality happily

61

uses all that assistance. He or she might not have excellent ideas on their own, but when showing naivety or making sexy gestures, everyone runs to help. Old time motion picture stars like Mary Pickford or Pearl White are good examples of actors who portrayed characters that were unfortunate victims, and gained through the help or intervention of others.

Short eyebrows.

Short eyebrows go together with a challenging personality. Short brows make you look younger than you are, and mostly give the impression that you are not only a very determined person, but also a hot lover. A person with short eyebrows is ready for challenges and he or she usually meets them easily. Very often fame and distinction strongly emerge when this person is young; however, a hot temper and talking without thinking are parts of his or her life, and can slowly extinguish a good reputation. The same goes for personal relationships and love affairs; they are fast, hot and memorable, but never last long.

Straight eyebrows.

Straight eyebrows illustrate a calm state of mind and physical power. This person has everything in good order in his or her life. In most cases a top administrative career is best for them. In relationships he or she clearly dominates. A spouse with straight eyebrows is not the warmest partner or lover, but can keep things well organized. When faced with a decision, this person selects work or other duties over family or friends. This discipline helps the individual to achieve superb results in sports or other hobbies. In many cases this person marries only to increase his or her social position.

Angular eyebrows.

Angular eyebrows are a part of the face of an adventurous person. He or she is very creative and most often also very famous for some public work. People like this have no restrictions around them, and if there is a wall somewhere, they will climb right over. Lack of restrictions often applies to marriage or other partnerships. Fooling around, trying new partners and enjoying life anywhere brings them excitement and adventure. We often find people with this feature in situations dealing with imagination, creativity and big, risky decisions: the stock market, sports, advertising, top military positions, and politics. People with much weaker skills often admire, and sometimes dream of marrying these exciting, prominent figures, although any marriages that do actually occur rarely last.

Round Eyebrows.

No matter which line of business they work in, people with round eyebrows usually succeed very well. You may see these people especially in real estate or any other market with high profits, as they love earning and keeping a lot of money. You may also meet a few celebrities with round eyebrows, and they are usually the ones that make a lot of money and, different from many others, they know how to invest their earnings. As a partner for life, especially in older years, they offer security, prudently safeguarding their purses.

****

In addition to the basic shapes, there are many special-shaped eyebrows:

New-Moon Eyebrows look as if they have been shaped even when they are not. They indicate a very successful and kind person, often from a happy family with many children. This person will rarely run into problems, and when he or she does, everything goes fine.

Lion Eyebrows is the name for powerfully thick, curved and strong eyebrows. If the eyes are also large, this individual can achieve a very good position.

Half-Moon Eyebrows indicate a person who is friendly and can socialize easily and meets interesting people.

Willow Eyebrows are very thin and curved and their owner is smart, alert and romantic. Sometimes he or she tends to be too smart and gets into trouble.

Weedy Eyebrows have an irregular shape, and their owner is usually not clear-headed and may not achieve fame or a high reputation.

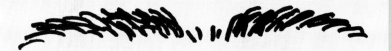

Joined Eyebrows belong to the militant and aggressive individual who has little control over anger. This person may succeed in sports and in other competitive fields.

Wispy eyebrows indicate lack of vitality and lack of ability to exercise authority over anyone, even oneself. The person is unable to form lasting relationships and is often sexually promiscuous.

Elizabeth Taylor

This is an oval-shaped face. People with this face shape are usually very attractive. The eyebrows are perfectly arched, showing fame, intelligence and creativity at a very early age. The eyes are very intent and interestingly balanced, indicating a very talented person.

THE EYES

The eyes represent the inner energy, Yin and Yang, intelligence, creativeness and vitality. Many face readers consider the eyes the most important part of the face. Not only do the eyes perform as important recipients of information and images, they also reflect the character and inner feelings of the owner. The ideal eyes are large, full and well set with the space of one eye-width between the eyes. That shows that the person is intelligent, people-friendly and very often artistic. If those eyes are on the face of a mother, it often reveals that rather than taking care of her children, she prefers hiring a nanny and focusing her interests outside the home.

When studying the size of the eyes, please keep in mind the overall measurements of the face. Large eyes on a large face are totally normal, but large eyes on a small face tell another story: the owner may be artistic, sensitive and outgoing, but often too outgoing to be a good mother. Small eyes—on a large face—show a person who is difficult to get to know. If the eyes are deep set, it suggests that the person is a romantic dreamer, intellectual and good at money matters. Sometimes the owners can become lost in fantasy in their youth and middle years and become too unrealistic to deal with the world

A small eye.

around them. If the eyes are protruding, this individual takes chances and is always looking for an opportunity to venture in a new direction.

Normally there's a space of one eye-width between the eyes. If they are much closer, that person has a very strong temper, but is also easily led. That

A protruding eye.

person sometimes even without noticing it easily judges other people, their manners and life. Eyes that are further away from each other reveal that the person has excellent taste and he or she has a magical gift for solving problems.

An eye with a lot of white under the iris.

Based on thousands of years of Chinese studies, the best eyes are those that have an iris large enough that the white of the eye is not visible above and below the iris. If there is a lot of white around the iris, that person may be adventurous, and he or she leads a wild life. Don't challenge that person, because he or she can really throw a fit, even a violent one, when challenged.

The color of the eyes is one thing everyone pays a lot of attention to. The meanings of the different eye colors vary depending on who is doing the reading. In general, brown eyes are considered trustworthy and ready to defend whatever belongs to them. This is especially true if the color is very dark brown. People with blue eyes usually make good lovers, and unless they live too much in the make-believe world, they are fairly happy with their lives. Green eyes divulge wisdom, friendliness and a giving person. This person is ready to give his or her life for a loved-one, and because of that same strong emotion, you had better not create any reason for jealousy. Grey-eyed people are usually intelligent. They know how to handle money matters and even emotional feelings. Overall, they are very stable, trustful people.

When reading the eyes, you should pay attention to the size, location and how much white is visible. Since we are looking into the internal energies of that person, the eyes reveal the most important facts of him or her. Everyone who has experienced a close friend or relative fading away after a lengthy illness knows how the eyes show the first signs of dying, much before the physical body is ready to give up.

*Tears are
the noble language of the eye.*

Robert Herrick

Lion Eyes are large with a strong focus. And their owner is a powerful person who is honest and straightforward and lives a long, successful life.

Tiger Eyes are very round and short and the irises have gold flecks. Again, they indicate a wealthy and powerful person with a very strong character, but only after the age of forty.

Cat Eyes are round with an interesting glitter and have a yellowish shine. This person is magnetic and influences others. He or she loves beauty and spending money and is very self-indulgent.

Ox Eyes are large and round with large pupils and very long, thick and straight lashes. They belong to very good, patient and pleasant people who enjoy long lives.

Elephant Eyes are long with a shape like a double lid above and below. These people enjoy pleasure, are reasonably successful and live a long life.

Monkey Eyes are deep set and dark and they move around a lot. These people tend to look and learn. They may be too conservative and worry too much.

Betty White

The eyes are very bright, meaning she is very clear headed. The nose is strong, so she has a certain amount of strength and domineering qualities. The upper lip is somewhat thin and the lower lip thicker, which shows she might enjoy a good debate. And the cheekbones are high, indicating the quality of authority even though the overall expression she gives out shows much sweetness.

Susan Sarandon

*Here we can see eyes that are slightly protruding.
A person with eyes like these is often very
unpredictable, and eager to take risks. This face
reveals strong emotions, and the person—no matter
how large the risks are—usually comes out the winner.*

TIIE NOSE

After the eyes, the next thing on the face that we look at is the nose. Perhaps this is the reason why a great number of cosmetic surgeries are performed on the nose, sometimes making it larger, sometimes smaller. A few years ago people wanted a nose with visible nostrils, but luckily that fad has passed. In Physiognomy we concentrate on the nose that we were born with, whatever that reveals. For instance, a person whose nostrils originally were visible is usually fairly liberal and generous, but also a blabbermouth to whom you should never tell any secrets.

The nose represents wealth and achievement in career as well as an ability to accumulate or waste wealth. Thus, a prominent, large nose is considered an asset to wealth and success. The location of the nose, in the middle zone of the face, mostly informs about achievements that take place in the middle of the person's life. Nevertheless, the effect of the nose carries through to the senior years.

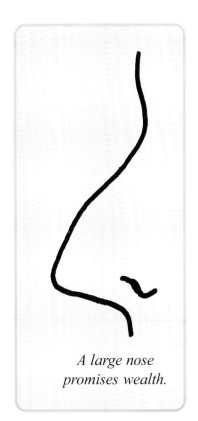

*A large nose
promises wealth.*

A nose long and straight, evenly built from top to bottom, features a person with an excellent career, happy family life, and very good health in the middle years and even longer. The end of the nose is round, as are the nostrils that are only slightly visible. Usually a person with a straight nose is trustful and extremely understanding. He or she sticks to whatever has been decided, and why not? Those goals are usually achieved. If the end of the nose also continues further down, making the nose look extremely long, that person is good at making wise decisions. He or she does not approve of any get-rich-quick schemes. Everything has to be logical and sensible. Even if you think this person is almost perfect, often the problem is this individual forgets not all people are as logical as he or she.

A long and straight nose brings an excellent career, happy family life, and good health.

An aquiline nose predicts wealth, power and fame.

If someone calls you hook-nosed, that is an immense compliment. The person with an aquiline nose has almost everything: excellent human relations, health, wealth, power and fame. And that person can enjoy these gifts until very old. You could really say that a nose like that is a money nose. Very often you see people with that feature in the leading business and political offices. And, a person with a nose like that, hardly ever needs Viagra!

If the nose is small, it shows this person enjoys life and is sociable, open-minded and outgoing. Rarely does a person with a small nose know how to get rich and the short concentration span may reflect also on human relationships. Then again, he or she is the most warmhearted person, who shouldn't care less about tomorrow.

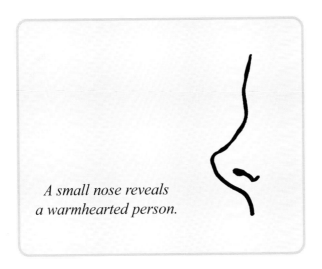

*A small nose reveals
a warmhearted person.*

If the nose is thin and bony, its owner is often self-centered, hypercritical and perfectionist. His or her biggest problem is that nobody wants to be with company like that; unfortunately that includes money!

*A big nose never spoiled
a handsome face.*

French proverb.

Jane Curtin

The nose is slightly small for the whole composition of her face, which means this person might suffer some health problems in the middle years. The face is slightly squarish, so it is a combination of Earth and Gold. It is a good combination because Earth feeds Gold, causing Gold, which is the creative part, to excel. The chin is strong, so she is a strong person.

Dragon Nose is the best kind of nose to have. Its owner gets everything including power and wealth.

Lion Nose shows an individual who is hardworking and can build a business empire. The nose is large, but the nostrils are not exposed.

Tiger Nose helps its owner to become famous, build a nice name and have an excellent home and family. This nose has a straight bridge, but is basically rounded.

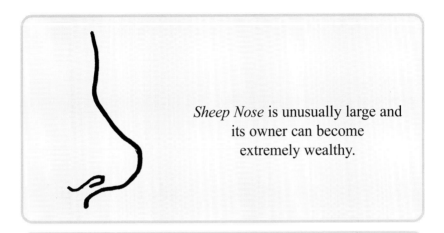

Sheep Nose is unusually large and its owner can become extremely wealthy.

Deer Nose is slightly flat, the root is narrow and the peak is rounded, not long or bony. This person is very kind and gets out of trouble easily, has a long life and will be successful in later years.

Monkey Nose is small and set very close to the upper lip. The nostrils are very flat. This person does not accumulate much money. The temperament is doubtful and its owner will find it hard to accomplish great success.

Dustin Hoffman

The nose is very strong and it is a very accumulative nose. The ears are very good and show that he has a kind disposition, but at the same time he is not a very easygoing person because his mouth is very tight. The lips are very thin indicating he is very determined and stubborn. His philtrum, the groove between the nose and the mouth, is very deep and shows he is a very sexy person.

THE MOUTH

The mouth represents the personality and emotional nature. For instance, performers and public speakers create with their mouths the impression people get from them. The lips may utter lies, but the way they are used reveals the carrier's character, sensuality and sexuality. A good mouth looks moist and rose red. A person with dry, colorless lips typically has a lack of energy and no gift of communication.

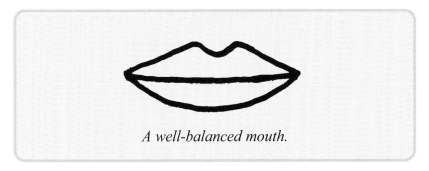

A well-balanced mouth.

If a person's mouth corners turn up even when that individual is not laughing, he or she is very optimistic, a great partner in the family and a good lover. If the lips look like a crescent, that person offers the very best company. That person will glow with energy and youth, even in old age. Everyone likes this individual, enjoys his or her pleasant company.

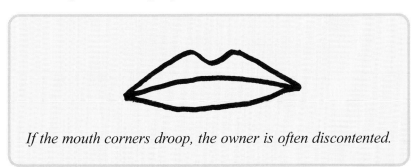

If the mouth corners droop, the owner is often discontented.

Then again, if the mouth corners droop, the owner is discontented and will make greedy demands. That person is never satisfied with anything or anyone, including himself. Also, if that person's lips are very thin and tight, you will most likely find extreme stubbornness, too. Don't take an individual like that to a fancy restaurant and don't bother offering him or her the best you can do; most likely your date will find too many things wrong or dissatisfying. Neither of you will enjoy the get-together. If the lips are thin but wide, the person likes to take command and boss others around.

Lips that are slightly open all the time reveal the open-mindedness of that person in many areas, including sex, new relationships and new ideas. On the other hand, a person with curved lips usually is very self-centered, who cares little what other people think. This individual may well be more interested in personal pleasures than personal friends. If a person's mouth turns up at the corners, it shows a cheerful and optimistic attitude and a great sense of humor.

He, from whose lips divine persuasion flows.

Homer

This is what some special-shaped mouths tell:

Dragon Mouth represents extreme fortune and good life. The lips are full, the corners are clear, and the outline is slightly square.

Tiger Mouth is so large that its owner can almost put his or her fist into it. It is large and broad with large lips. The owners of these mouths are usually powerful people with a rich, long life and lots of money.

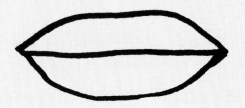

Ox Mouth is also large, but the lips are thick and straight. These people are pleasant with warm personality.

Monkey Mouth lips are long and thin and have lots of lines in the middle. These people are very careful with money, but they enjoy long, healthy lives.

Shirley MacLaine

*These lips are called crescent lips. The mouth turns up at
the corners and has a cheerful look. Crescent-mouthed
people laugh a lot, smiling even at bad luck, and they are
highly sensitive. They have a good sense of humor and
are fun to be around. The face is heart-shaped, a
combination of Water and Wood. Water feeds Wood,
making her mind work quickly.*

CHAPTER FOUR:
SEVEN OTHER FEATURES

The Forehead
The Cheekbones
The Jawbones
The Chin
The Philtrum
The Under Eye
The Laugh Lines

The forehead, under-eye area, cheekbones, laugh lines, jawbone, chin and the philtrum (the groove between the nose and mouth) represent forces that may strengthen or limit your potential. When the major features on our face—which we more or less can control and adjust—tell about the possibilities we have during our lives; these seven other features are something that we usually have no control over. Studying those helps us understand each other, and ourselves, and it gives assistance in making the right decisions, the correct choices.

The following table offers the basic view of these features.

OTHER FEATURES	AFFECTS TO
forehead	character
cheekbones	power and energy
jawbones	status in society
chin	strength and survival
philtrum	sexuality and productivity
under eye	fertility and quality of children
laugh lines	longevity and quality of life

THE FOREHEAD

The forehead represents character, and what we get from our background: education and parental guidance or principles that have been instilled. The height of the forehead has its significant meanings. A high forehead is a sign of that person has or has had a good relationship with his or her parents. Often the first child of the family has the highest forehead, and he or she most likely got the best care and advice from the parents. If another child, not the oldest, has a high forehead, he or she most likely has to help and support the parents, often at a fairly young age. If the forehead is both high and square, it indicates a good intellectual ability with a fine family background. Overall, people with high foreheads are very intelligent and able to solve great puzzles by themselves. If the height goes to the extreme of being higher than one third of the face, that person may well be totally sunken into his or her own thoughts and puzzles, thus staying far away from the reality of life.

Normally in face reading, if you find negative characteristics in your own or someone else's face, bear in mind that if other facial features are good or average they balance almost everything. That is especially if there have been problems in the youth, but if the rest of the face has better features, that person most likely will have a much better adulthood. When reading the forehead, however, the reading should reflect on the whole forehead, because the shape and width may disclose their own details also.

A forehead that narrows going up, often seen on the faces of Fire people, uncovers the person's interest in excitement. A person with a square forehead is often spiritually gifted, but if the shape is also long, you may have marriage problems. A square, but very high forehead, may reveal becoming a widow at a rather early age. A round and tall forehead is an indication of a very calm person who hardly ever loses his or her temper. Most likely, this person's childhood was very pleasant and easy, which is why he or she does not worry much about anything as an adult.

A forehead that narrows going up, often seen on the faces of Fire people, uncovers the person's interest in excitement.

Luke Perry

The very high forehead shows that he has achieved a great deal of fame and accomplishment at a very early age. The eyes and eyebrows are good, so he will maintain his ability up to his middle years, but later he may gradually fade away from the scene. The element is Wood.

THE CHEEKBONES

The cheekbones represent power, the amount of masculine Yang energy within a couple and a family, but also in public appearance and the business world. In personal relationships, the partner with the stronger cheekbones will become the dominant spouse and parent. In most cases well-developed cheekbones are the basis, almost a requirement, to achieve top power positions in business and politics. This also applies to leading positions in science, sports and the entertainment industry. On some faces, even though the cheekbones are strong and high, they are not clearly visible. For instance, a person with Water element has the cheekbones hidden under his or her facial tissues, and that is why a Water person is an excellent negotiator in face-to-face meetings, or poker-playing for high stakes. As we know, when we bite our teeth together, a change can be seen around our cheekbones. If they are not visible, we are already half way home as a winner.

Reese Witherspoon

A heart-shaped face, which is a combination of Water and Wood. This face is broader in the forehead area than in the chin area. And the high cheekbones tell that she is the one who says where the dinner table stands. The laugh lines are long and curve in below the mouth, indicating a long life but possible loneliness at the end.

THE JAWBONES

The jawbones represent status, the position one achieves in life. The location, the lowest third of the face, in the bottom zone, advises that their meaning is the strongest beyond the age of fifty. When studying the jawbones, remember to keep them separate from the chin itself, as they each have their own meanings. Ideally the jawbones are evenly formed, approximately the same width as the forehead. The bottom corners of the jawbones can be seen looking somewhat round, and not too strong and massive. A person with this jawbone structure usually obtains a lot of respect. He or she is very stubborn, self-centered and proud, the one who always gets what he or she wants, and easily finds the best position and clout in society.

Then again a person with jawbones that become narrower toward the chin, and which end up a very small chin, cannot be praised. Often that person has a strong forehead, which may expose the gift of spirituality and good nature—but when the face clearly gets much narrower going down, he or she should especially pay a lot of attention in old age to his or her health. This person may have multiple gifts and qualities, but because of health problems—sometimes hidden at the early stages—he or she is rarely successful.

Demi Moore

If a woman has a strong jaw line, she is a doer and not a homemaker. She may have a lot of children, but she can still go out and do well in her career. Her eyebrows are wonderful, so she can achieve fame at a very early age. The eyes are pretty and very dreamy and creative. The ears are good. Basically, she has a kind heart.

THE CHIN

The chin is a symbol of strength. When studying the chin, in the bottom zone, pay attention to its shape—whether it is round or square or sharp-pointed, and if it is straight or protruding. Even when the chin is in its senior years' zone, it still represents the person's strength. Ideal is a sturdy, round-edged chin, whose owner will have energy until the very end, staying healthy and welcoming his or her children, grandchildren and even great-grandchildren into this world.

Square outlines on the chin reveal stubbornness. The owner may well stay healthy, but because of his or her difficult character, old years' are moody and melancholy. If the chin is protruding, such a person may be aggressive and prefers to fight. The receding chin indicates one who is somehow poor of strength and most likely will not live a fully content life. Some people consider a cleft in the chin very sexy, most likely because some famous, old film stars had them. And that is what the cleft tattles, a person who loves being the center of everything that happens in a room and is blindly attracted to flattery and admiration. Inside, that person is like a family's only child, who must have all the attention.

Mick Jagger

An interesting face! The mouth is fairly large, so the owner is good-hearted but needs to do things his way. The mouth corners turn up, meaning happiness and optimism. The laugh lines are very long; he is going to live a long life. When the laugh lines are deep, it is associated with sexual activity. So are a large mouth with full lips, high cheekbones, protruding ears, a long nose that points down, a strong chin, and shadows under the eyes.

THE GROOVE BETWEEN THE NOSE AND THE MOUTH—THE PHILTRUM

The groove between the nose and the mouth indicates sexuality and productivity in spiritual life, work and hobbies. It joins the nose, which—according to the Chinese studies—represents man's sexual organ, and the mouth, which represents the comparable organ in a woman. Even though this groove expresses its carrier's sexuality for both sexes—the stronger and longer, the more sex-driven—you should pay special attention to a man's groove between the nose and the mouth. In a normal-size man's face, the groove ideally is one inch long. This indicates that life's elixir, including the sexual stamina, will endure throughout life. If the groove is deep, it gives reassurance to the fact that the man in question is capable of producing a large family. If the groove is shallow and short, almost unnoticeable, his interest most likely lies elsewhere, not in the bedroom. Men or women, whose grooves seem to disappear before the upper lip, should not depend on earning their livelihood in business, at least not anywhere where they are directly dealing with public. For some reason, very few people wish to finalize business deals with a person carrying a groove such as that.

It is interesting that already the ancient Greeks considered the area between the nose and the mouth an erotic symbol, and a measurement of sexual potency. The proper English name, philtrum, originates from the same root as the word philter—love stimulant, philanthropy—charity and philanderer—a man who has extramarital affairs. Checking the philtrum area of the face is very easy—normally it is openly visible—and given that it is normal to look at a person's mouth when he or she is speaking, most people don't even know that you are reading the philtrum. Keep that in mind when selecting a partner for work, life, or sex.

A beautiful face is admired even when its owner doesn't say anything.

Danish proverb.

Barbra Streisand

If the groove is flat or shallow, it indicates one whose interests are likely to be elsewhere rather than in sexual activity. The forehead is rounded and shows she is a highly intelligent person. The eyes are very close set, indicating she is very protective. In a way, she likes to close everything so that she is not exposing herself to the world. The nose is strong, making her a capable person business-wise and in personal matters. The lips are interesting because the upper lip is little thicker than the lower lip. People with this feature usually are self-oriented. They do whatever they please and they are not going to worry about other people's opinions, suggestions or even advice.

There comes a time in every woman's life when the only thing that helps is a glass of champagne.

Bette Davis

THE UNDER-EYE AREA

The under-eye area reveals fertility, the number of offspring—in the future or past—and the quality of the children. It also reveals the person's willingness to make children. When the philtrum represents its owner's sexual qualities, abilities and activities, the under-eye area discloses the results of those activities. If a man wishes to have healthy children and a mother that takes good care of them, he should choose a woman whose under-eye area is full, like a silkworm's cocoon, and light in color. Even though, according to Western medicine, black under-eyes may alert of a health problem, in many cultures that is a sign of a person who goes to bed for something other than sleeping. Physiognomy describes that if the area is dark and sunken, it indicates infertility as well as a restrained and pessimistic view of life.

Leonardo DiCaprio

This is a heart-shaped face and usually a heart-shaped face belongs to a woman. They are very kind-hearted. They have a kind of feminine side in them; they are very nurturing. The eyebrows are dominant so he is capable of achieving fame in the theatre, the arts or anything that brings him before the public.

THE LAUGH LINES

This is an easy feature in face reading, since the laugh lines are visible on most people's faces. They start from somewhere on the sides of the nostrils and end up above or below the sides of the mouth. The laugh lines represent longevity and good health. They exist from birth, but most of the time, unless you are smiling, they will show up after forty years of life. If they are visible when the person is not smiling and under forty, that individual will have various problems, mostly health related.

What can we learn about them? That one who laughs a lot lives longer? Long laugh lines that continue lower than the sides of the mouth indicate a long, healthy life. If the laugh lines curve into the corners of the mouth, it indicates poverty or poor health in old age.

In Western culture, the average lifespan is around 75 years, or somewhat more. Chinese culture dictates that a person's life is fulfilled when he or she has seen not only the children and grandchildren grown, but also one or more generations after that. That means that he or she is expected to live more than ninety years!

Long laugh lines indicate a long, healthy life.

Renee Zellweger

There is a lot of Water in this face. She is flexible like water in nature. Water finds its way wherever it is. Water makes life possible and rich. Water accumulates and so does a Water person: She adapts easily to new situations and comes out wealthier. Gold is a perfect pair choice for the Water personality.

CHAPTER FIVE:
OTHER FACIAL FEATURES

Horizontal Forehead Lines
Vertical Forehead Lines
Crow's Feet
The Eye Lids and the Wrinkles on the Lips
Hair and Beard
Eyelashes and Moles
Health and Face
Other Faces and Features...

There are countless other, smaller features on the face that reveal certain facts about that person. For instance, the way the hair or the beard grows, moles on the face, and the various directions and numbers of the lines on the forehead, the wrinkles at the corners of and around the eyes, old-age wrinkles on the upper lip, etc. They are all equally important details in face reading.

We have two ears and one mouth that we may listen the more and talk the less.

Zeno

Britney Spears

This is an oblong face, which the Chinese thought to be in a perfect balance. It belongs to the Gold category. Gold people enjoy good fortune with little effort. She should marry somebody who has an Earth-shaped or Water-shaped face. Earth would provide realism and strength this element needs. Water and Gold are a good combination even though Water benefits more than Gold from this pairing.

THE HORIZONTAL FOREHEAD LINES

Horizontal forehead lines are considered fortunate. If there is one line and it is high crossing the forehead, it can help bring success. If the line is high up, it tells that the person had to start working already at a very early age, and later on in his or her life, there will be a lot of success. If the only line is located very low, it means that the carrier has to go through a lot of obstacles in his or her life.

Two horizontal lines are considered extremely favorable, meaning high intelligence. Not only is the person clever, but the results are excellent. He or she is bright, cultured and presentable. If there are three horizontal lines, you don't need to be clever or bright. Life is kind to you and good fortune falls in your lap. But— don't get too excited—more than three horizontal lines tell that the person's energy is strong, wanting to gather information from all over, but also dividing his or her attention into so many different matters that after a while nothing succeeds and people start thinking of him or her as a village fool.

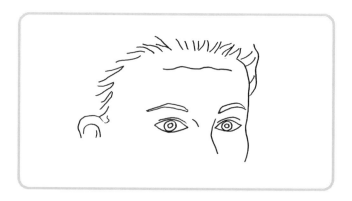

One line high crossing the forehead can help bring success.

Liberace

This face has a broad forehead and a pointed chin and it is a typical Wood face. Wood people usually are very creative, very idealistic and sometimes they live in a dream world. He has two very deep dimples and it means he is admired by a lot of people. The nose is strong and this person likes monetary gains and accumulating possessions.

THE VERTICAL LINES BETWEEN THE EYEBROWS

The person with only one vertical line between the eyebrows is usually a person who worries too much. It is normal that the person is very intelligent—often a writer of some kind—and the beginning of his or her life is very promising. However, in many cases, no plans will be fulfilled; it looks like that person is only able to concentrate on one thing at a time.

Two vertical lines between the eyebrows are normal and considered fortunate. Three are even better. More than three, just like the horizontal lines on the forehead, are not so lucky, and the person can never go through with his or her imaginative plans.

*Two vertical lines between the eyebrows
are considered fortunate.*

Harvey Keitel

This is a very serious face, and, as you can see, there is a line in the middle of the eyebrows. That is called a suspending needle. The person with such a line is likely to get off to a talented start, but expectations are not fulfilled. Many tensions and pressures often plague this person, although he or she is likely to be intellectually superior. Writers often have suspending needles. Especially if you see that the mouth is very tight, the person is somewhat disappointed. Even though he has accomplished a great deal, he still feels like an under-achiever.

THE WRINKLES OUTSIDE THE EYES

The lines at the outer corners of the eyes are called crow's feet because they resemble the three digits of a crow's foot. They are the signs of a faithful—or not so faithful—marriage and the person's ability to stay committed. On the face of an elderly person those lines don't have a specific meaning but, if a young person— under the age of thirty—has them, they most certainly are worth analysis. Many crinkles indicate sexual overindulgence. The corner of the left eye indicates the number of marriages and the right corner extramarital affairs.

When seriously dating a young person with an intention to marry him or her, you definitely should pay attention to these wrinkles. If there are a lot of them—at the corner of either eye— that person most likely is not ready for a faithful, long-lasting relationship. Multiple wrinkles uncover the desires of multiple sexual experiments—and not with just one partner!

A young person, who has "crow's feet" in the corner of his or her right eye, may be interested in extramarital affairs.

THE EYELIDS AND THE WRINKLES ON THE LIPS

A horizontal line on the eyelid is fairly normal, meaning good, whereas multiple lines either above or below the eye tell about the person's suspicious and super-careful nature. The horizontal line under the nose means the person tends to be dominating. And a line that follows down the nose is a sign of a person working very hard, but who cannot always hold on to well-earned money.

On the lips of a young person, the horizontal lines on the upper lip show self-centeredness and a propensity to isolate oneself. Those lines on the upper lip of an elderly person reveal that he or she should pay special attention to health.

THE HAIR AND THE BEARD

Physiognomy studies the hair based on its quality, amount and form, as well as based on the color and shininess. According to the Chinese scrutiny, the ideal hair is dark, half coarse, fairly thick, straight and shiny; however, not too oily and not too straight. A person with that kind of hair has intelligent, ambitious ideas and he or she achieves very much during the years and lives an incredibly contented life.

A person with very strong hair may be hot-tempered and stubborn. You really should be careful when engaging in a deep conversation with this individual. If the person's hair is naturally thick and strong, it can mean that he or she is over-reactive and over-emotional. This is the case especially if the hair is extremely thick. Because of the person's strong emotions and feelings, this human being sometimes reacts overly strong and the emotional life may lack many of the unique features that are quite normal to other people. Hair like that on the head of a large-boned, large-headed person causes no problems, but on the head of a small-sized person it may be chaotic. He or she is not able to maintain the internal balance and comprehend the realities of normal life. That is why achieving life's good results can be almost impossible. This person's dreams of a long and prosperous life will never be fulfilled.

The hair with fine texture reveals the owner's very delicate and artistic internal emotions, wisdom and peacefulness; however, a person like that does not always reach the goals one sets for one's self. Emotionally this individual is far too sensitive, too fragile, even too shy. What is missing is the aggressiveness needed to bring out his or her strong inner self.

If the hair is very fine or very weak, that is the sign of the person lacking life force. He or she might have energy in the earlier years, but in the adult years that energy rapidly vanishes. Especially in the last remaining years of his or her life, when all initiative and self-confidence are gone, this person really loves being flattered, no matter how empty.

The Chinese face readers, over thousands of years—themselves mostly with straight, black hair—consider the curly hair's owner intelligent and clever, but very stubborn and unpredictable. Just a few curls here and there bring to light the tendency to have a high temper or eagerness to tell racy jokes. If the head is full of strong curls, the person is irresponsible and unreliable; an individual who bathes in self-centeredness.

Chinese studies of Physiognomy assure that black is the best color of the hair, because it represents life's energy and good health. Fair hair expresses a weak person, a "yes-man" who does not have an opinion of his or her own. This person is not good company.

Donald Sutherland

A longish face indicates that he carries a lot of Wood in his make-up, and that shows he is a very idealistic person. The interesting thing is that the eyebrows go up at the corners, which is a sign of someone who is combative, and always ready for a challenge. The ears are very large and well-set and show that the potential he has is very good.
He also will live a long time.

Red hair is—of course—a sign of temperament, of people who react too strongly to almost everything. A young person getting gray hair is most likely to meet with hardships later in life, but if your hair turns gray after the age of fifty, it merely shows that you have successfully met the major responsibilities in your life.

The length of the hair is obviously completely up to the individual; however, do remember that it is very important how others see you and read you. A long-haired person is generally considered good-tempered and peace loving, yet that person very often enjoys being the center of attention at social gatherings. A woman's long hair is a sign of loyalty and indicates she is a hard worker.

A receding hairline after the age of fifty shows that the person is developing spiritually, but early balding on a young person discloses his or her weakening ability and interest in sexual matters.

The same rules that we have for hair also apply for men's beards. The most positive kind of beard grows evenly and neatly and does not grow too high up on the cheeks. For many growing a beard is a cosmetic way to cover something on the face. One of them is a receding chin or jawbones. The moustache can also hide a lot, and especially the philtrum. This does not really make any sense—at least for a young man who has a striking groove between his nose and mouth!

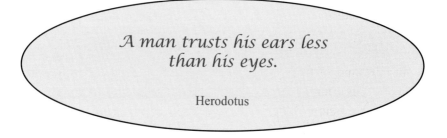

A man trusts his ears less than his eyes.

Herodotus

THE EYELASHES AND MOLES

Long eyelashes are part of the face of a creative, sensitive person, and then again the short ones belong to a practical, strong individual. If the lashes are very thin, weak, and they easily break, that person most likely has problems with his or her blood circulation and he or she tends to be lazy and sluggish. Please, remember that while wearing long false eyelashes will not make you creative and sensitive, they will change the impression other people will have of you.

Moles are an interesting and a very revealing group of features in Chinese face reading. Our clothing hides some of our moles, but some are very visible on the facial area. In most cases the moles on the other parts of the body have a good meaning, especially those under the soles of the feet. Facial moles can predict fortunate or unfortunate issues. Also, what is interesting is very often a mole on the face area has a twin on the part of the body the facial area represents.

A mole in the middle of the forehead is good for a profession, but not good for family life. The owner may become so violent that it hinders the marriage. A bright and light mole between the eyebrows divulges excellent opportunities in work life, and the knowledge and ability to use a very sophisticated and highly developed vocabulary. Moles in the eye area each have their own stories to tell. A person with a mole in the corner of the eyelid usually likes traveling and moving from place to place. Home for a long spell, the person becomes restless and unbalanced. If the mole is immediately below the outer corner of the eyelid, the person has strong urge for flirting and hunting for the opposite sex. Many cultures consider someone with that kind of mole sexy and romantic, but if you plan to have him or her as your partner, beware of potential philandering. A person with a mole below the inner corner of the eyelid should take good care of his or her health, as this mole may cause bad luck, especially in health.

Drew Barrymore

The upper and lower lips of this face are well balanced; they show equal fullness. These people smile easily and enjoy spontaneous laughter. The corners of her lips go up so she has a positive personality. The right eye is slightly smaller than the left. The right side of the face represents feminine Yin energy and the left side masculine Yang energy. When the left eye is larger than the right eye, it means she is a very aggressive person.

Moles on the cheek are signs of durability and strength, but very often persons with moles achieve the goals by sacrificing their relationships. The moles on the lower part of the cheek are often called Society Moles, and their owners happily indulge themselves in society organizations, balls and parties. The need to be seen with the right people in the right places is very important to that person, so emotional balance and family life often suffer. Moles above the lips often belong to a person that loves good food and drinks and happily bathes in all the good things in life. The nature is usually quite nice and considerate, but in the old age, this person may turn into an individual who is never satisfied with anything. A mole at the end of the chin may reveal a human being with a tendency to fuss around too much, often snooping in other people's private affairs. Moles in the ears are very desirable, as they predict success in family life, in business life and overall everywhere. A mole at the end of the nose, this is especially with men, foresees several healthy children to be born.

Scars on the face or other reasons for the facial skin to be broken are usually not considered desirable. The person should watch out for accidents and health concerns, especially in those areas where the disfigurements appear (remember the three horizontal zones). On the other hand, freckles are usually considered a good sign; they display a friendly person who has a lot of friends. In some cases, the freckles are also an indication of a strong sexual appetite.

Moles above the lips often belong to a person that loves good food and drinks.

George Clooney

An oblong face, a society face, so clearly this face is very fortunate. People adore a face like this. Good ears, too, so he obviously comes from a good family. The eyebrows are very bushy, showing he is a very intense person. The nose is slightly short. That means the person doesn't particularly want to take any kinds of responsibilities. The mouth, compared to the face size, is fairly small. That may reveal a person's rich fantasy life, plus a tendency to feel comfortable just being alone with his thoughts.

HEALTH AND FACE

In addition to what the face can tell about the past and future, it can also recommend taking a closer look at the present health of that person. The face is the first thing that any medical person looks at, no matter in which culture the patient is seeking help. Making full diagnoses by looking at a person's face, is another topic of the Chinese face reading, and in this book, we are only touching the surface. However, please keep in mind that a diagnose made using this information should always stay as a guidance only. Before any treatments, one should always consult a professional health care person.

Abnormalities in the area above the eyebrows often reflect problems in the gall bladder, bladder, liver and stomach. The eyebrows themselves show the overall amount of energy we have—of life, and sexuality. The stronger they are the better. Vertical lines going up from eyebrows suggest that one should pay attention to the liver and bladder. One vertical line in the middle of the eyebrows—as mentioned earlier—reveals a person who worries a lot. And because of that, he or she should pay attention to the condition of the stomach.

The half moon-shaped area directly below the eyes is also very informative. A darkish brown or grey color suggests liver, kidney and stomach problems, mostly caused by too rich food and/or too much alcohol. The areas below that, as well as the nose, reflect the condition of the heart and one should pay attention to any changes in the coloring of the skin. Strong lines running from the inner corners of the eyes down and to the sides of the mouth can project problems in the colon and the bowel movement. Note that the Laugh Lines usually start near the nostrils.

If the area on the sides of the nostrils and parts of the cheeks next to them start showing abnormal redness or puffiness, the condition of the lungs should be checked out. Discoloration or cracks on the lips advise of possible problems in the stomach or intestines.

*He who has health is rich
and does not know it.*

Italian proverb.

OTHER FACES AND FEATURES...

Jack Nicholson

A very interesting face, of course, especially the nose. As you can see, the nostrils are indeed flaring. That shows he is a very emotional and might throw a tantrum any time. The lips are thin even though he has a very wide smile. He is ready to say something anytime he wants to. The ears are good. They are long and nicely set so he is a very fortunate person.

Richard Gere

This face is a combination of Fire and Wood. It is a very interesting combination. The Fire is burning the Wood. This person is brilliant, but at the same time, if the Fire burns unattended, he could get into trouble. So he needs to balance that Fire within him to avoid going to extremes. The eyes are very shiny and much focused. The nose is generous so all his features are very, very good. He certainly has a great life. The only thing he needs to worry about is balancing his energies so he doesn't go haywire with them.

Nicholas Cage

This is a very typical Wood face. Wood-face people are very creative. They always want to do something new, something inventive. But the interesting thing here is that Wood people usually don't have such strong eyebrows, which shows that he is also a passionate Wood. Usually Wood people are quite down-to-earth, quite reserved. This person has a little bit of aggressiveness in him.

Harrison Ford

The oblong-shape face and the main elements are Gold and Wood. Very sharp eyes with very strong eyebrows. He is very physical and in a way masculine and aggressive. The nose is strong but tends to tilt on the right side slightly, showing this person has a lot of feminine trace. The mouth is open so he is also a very easy-going person. The top lip is very thin, the lower lip is quite full, meaning this person loves to discuss about any subject.

You can be young without money,
but you can't be old without it.

Elizabeth Taylor

Arnold Schwarzenegger

This is a rectangular face that belongs to Wood. The top part is very strong, very well balanced, and it shows good mental powers. He wants to take chances, but on his own, not depending on others. The eyebrows are strong and the eyes are focused. The nose is good. The lower part is a little weaker and it means he will lose some strength and stamina in the later part of his life.

Jennifer Lopez

*This is a heart-shaped face, meaning it has both
Water and Wood. The cheekbones are high so she is
a determined person. The cheekbones show power
in family life as well as in public life. The brows are
even and slightly upward, which tells about
the person's active lifestyle. She can be ambitious,
even aggressive; she is very outgoing
and loves to travel.*

People who are very beautiful make their own laws.

Vivien Leigh.

Meg Ryan

This is a diamond-shape face, which is a combination of Wood and Fire. It is a good combination because Wood helps Fire. She is more out-going than the pure Wood type is. The eyes are very pretty, very soft, very feminine. I think she is a sweet lady with the pleasant disposition. The nose is fine and the mouth is also very balanced.

Whoopi Goldberg

This is a very interesting face. It's really an oval shape but carries Water in combination, which basically means two things. Gold and Water means she is elegant but also very wise. The eyes are very large and far separated and shows that she is very smart and quick-minded. The nose is fine and has a round tip so she can balance herself very well. The mouth is generous and shows that she has a lot of personality.

136

He had the sort of face that, once seen, is never remembered.

Oscar Wilde

Kiefer Sutherland

The top part of the face shows this person started out his professional life quite early and could have achievement at a very early age. But then again a person with these features may be rather indulgent and probably is a little bit self-centered and therefore gets into a lot of trouble. The lobe of the left ear may reveal problems around six years of age. The pointed chin can show narrowness of viewpoint. Also, special attention should be given to health matters in maturity.

A good many women are good tempered simply because it saves the wrinkles coming too soon.

Baroness Von Hutten

Queen Latifah

The eyes are very sensuous, and so are the lips, which basically means she is a very sensuous lady. The nose shows that she is a very emotional person, and perhaps slightly temperamental. There is some Fire element in the face and that makes her outgoing, exciting, temperamental and restless. There is never a dull moment with her.

140

A yawn is at least an honest opinion.

Farmer's Almanac, 1966

Tom Hanks

A Wood element is very strong in this face. Often the forehead is high and the ears and the nose can be long. He is creative and wise. The Wood people see farther and in a broader range than others. They are spiritual and honest, but sometimes their head is in the clouds.

John Goodman

This is a very open and interesting face. It belongs to Fire and it is a little bell-shaped, narrow on top, slightly larger on jawbone area. The eyes reveal a very humorous person. At the same time the eyebrows tend to come down a little bit, which means that he is out to please the world and everybody. The mouth is small. Even he is trying to please everybody, he has got a very strong mind of his own and is not going to tolerate any kind of nonsense.

Sylvester Stallone

All the features slant down on this person. The eyebrows droop, the corner of the eyes slant, and the lips curve down. This is a very cynical person in some ways. But at the same time he is laughing at the world and everybody he is with. He doesn't take everything seriously and he does whatever he pleases.

Mel Gibson

An oblong face again, a Gold personality of a society person. Obviously he will achieve a very high status in society. The eyes are very mischievous, and the eyebrows tend to droop down. When the eyebrows tend to come down, it means that these individuals would like to please those around them. The corners of his lips do go up so he is a very positive person. The ears are well-formed so he is a very fortunate person.

A red nose is caused by sunshine or moonshine.

Evan Esar

Jim Carrey

The Wood element is very dominant in this face. And what is interesting is that the chin is also very strong. Usually Wood people have a small chin and it would mean that old days are not very good. But if your chin is as strong as his, your old days are quite comfortable. We can see from his eyes that he is a romantic dreamer, intellectual and good at money matters. His ears tell that he is adventures and likes to go his own way.

CHAPTER SIX: CLOSING

What the Others Say
Conclusion
Final Words
About the Authors
More Information

WHAT THE OTHERS SAY

Chinese face reading dates back at least 2,500 years. During that period of time, many—not only the Chinese—have adjusted and changed their interpretations of the facial features, each based on their own, individual studies. This book reveals one portion, one discipline of those studies, one that we have found to be incredibly accurate and fascinating. There are many other publications, written throughout the years, offering different or similar instructions and advice, most of them reaching the very same conclusions. This applies to many other ancient Chinese studies, too, many of which have the academic stature of Western science. Acupuncture is certainly one of the most well-known ones.

Western medicine does not outright approve the studies of Chinese face reading. After all, there's been no way to test and prove the meanings of human facial features in a laboratory environment that Western science likes. And yet, in the Western world, when a patient visits a doctor's office, the first, basic signs are read from the patient's face and eyes, as well as the color of the skin and lips. The shape and size of the head, together with the whole body, reveal facts that schools of psychology have known for hundreds of years. By our own experiences, we know that a narrow-faced person with a slim and tall body structure behaves differently than someone with a round face and a stubby, heavy-built body. And many Western medical doctors confirm that they make observations on potential psychological illnesses from the forehead of the patient.

The difference in faraway cultures is enormous. For example, a Western M.D. often begins examination of the patient by checking the pulse's speed and strength, then follows with laboratory tests and numerous state-of-the-art electronic equipment. In most cases—after waiting a few hours to several days for the results—they help the doctor diagnose the illness. The Western doctor's Chinese colleague also checks the patient's pulse, studies the face and—in

Gwyneth Paltrow

This face has a lot of Earth element in it. Earth people need a secure home and they often stay in one place. They are still, patient and stable. Their word is their bond. An Earth person often marries another Earth type even though a better partner would be one who has Fire in his face.

most cases within a few minutes—tells the patient the detailed diagnosis.

Besides China, face reading has been studied and developed in other countries, too. One very interesting method was created in California, USA, at the beginning of the twentieth century. Mr. Edward Jones, a judge in a California courthouse, reported observations on thousands of people who came to his courtroom. The face reading method he created is called Personology, and those studies were further improved by Mr. Robert Whiteside, who in the 1950s performed detailed studies on the faces of thousands more individuals. The findings of the two gentlemen very much support the findings of Chinese face reading. They, too, found that people with thin hair are more sensitive than people with thick hair, or that those with big noses have a better understanding of money. The biggest difference is that in addition to the facial features, shape and size, they also studied overall body structure, and the significance of genes and with them our inheritance from parents, grandparents and great grandparents.

And yet—all that can also be seen on the face.

PHYSIOGNOMY IN A NUTSHELL

The Face

In Physiognomy, the first thing to observe is the overall look, shape and size of the face, followed by the individual features. The first overall impression is very important, as it often stays with us for a long time. Most of us have experienced situations where we meet someone for the first time and either like or dislike that person immediately. The combination of the person's facial features, together with skin tones, creates the overall first impression.

Basic Elements

The second important feature to study on a face is the actual shape of the face. From that alone, we can discover if the individual is an ever-active Fire person, a respected and fascinating Gold character, an Earth element who is safe and secure to be with, an intelligent and foreseeing Wood person, or a wealthy and cooperative Water element. We should remember that the basic element of the face follows us from birth to death, and old age or changes in body weight—for instance—don't affect that fact. When studying the fundamental element of a person, and you clearly see the person has gained weight, you should deduct that addition to get the correct reading; and vice versa if the person has lost a lot of weight. The same rule applies after lengthy illness or a long life of very hard work.

Unfortunately, persons with only one easy-to-read facial element are rare. The faces with two or more elements combined are much more common, much more difficult to read, still, once you have been able to figure out the correct combination, the rest is easier.

John Travolta

This is what we call a combination of Fire and Wood. As you can see, the forehead is little narrow. The lower zone is a little broader, but at the same time it is longish, so that carries the Wood. The eyes are very brilliant. They are a slightly close set, meaning that he is sort of protective by nature. He wants to protect himself. He is afraid to be hurt but at the same time he wants to please everybody, as he has a very broad and happy smile. But the nose is very straight and shows he is honest with a lot of integrity. A good face!

CHAPTER SIX: CLOSING

Most Important Features

As soon as the element is read, we should carry forward to the different age zones and to the important features of the ears, eyebrows, eyes, nose and mouth. The ears are a good feature since they don't change very much during the years. Even though the actual face reading can start from after childhood, the ears reveal the time before that—from the mother's womb to the teenage years.

We can tell a lot from the person's eyebrows, as they expose the abilities to succeed in family, work and fame. It is said that the eyes are the windows of the soul, and they do inform so much of the person's intelligence and inner energy. The nose and the mouth speak out their story, the first one about our most important aspect of life—mid-life—and the second one about our emotional life and character.

Other Features

When all of the above are clear, the person doing the Physiognomy should concentrate on the forehead, which has youth and wisdom written all over it; the cheekbones tell their rules on who makes the rules; the jawbones and chin, forecasting the later years in life. The laugh lines on the sides of the mouth tell about our health and happiness in the senior years, the under-eye area, the size of our family, and the space between the nose and mouth, confidential sexual cravings.

The minor facial details are no less important: The horizontal lines of the forehead revealing the amount or lack of love in the youth, and the vertical lines exposing the person's strength, intelligence and cultural talents. The wrinkles at the outer corners of the eyes tell about the family life and the life outside the family, the wrinkles on the lips or the nose disclose additional information on the nature and health of that person. The moles have numerous secrets of their own, depending on where they are located, and even though the length, shape and color of the hair and beard are very much in our control, they still have their own telling words.

As for changing your features, such as hair or beard color, eyebrows, facelifts, nose jobs, etc., this does not change the real you. This has very little to do with pre-determining your future. Psychologically, cosmetic surgery may change the way you think about yourself, thus changing actions and reactions—and the future. Even more important, the alterations may adjust the way the others see, think and react toward you, reshaping your ways of life.

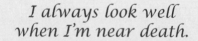

I always look well when I'm near death.

Greta Garbo

FINAL WORDS

Chinese face reading, or Physiognomy, is fascinating, and also very beneficial in many ways. No matter if it is practiced as entertainment with friends or as a serious study, Physiognomy can offer extremely interesting pieces of information about a human being. But what has this book given? Certainly we all know that a person with the corners of the mouth pointing down all the time is not a fully content human being. Of course the Chinese, in their studies, have noticed that, too, but in addition, we learn an endless amount of other details. Some of them we realize to be true right away, some only during the years to come.

If you already have read the whole book—including the very important photo and image captions—you have noticed that the main text and the captions go hand-in-hand, supporting each other. If you skipped a section, we strongly recommend that you go back and read the book again from cover to cover. Although full knowledge of Physiognomy is extremely broad and detailed, we have given you all the basics, and in some areas even much more. From this point on, one could easily continue for years. For instance, it is possible to study a detailed reading of the face, for each year of the person's life, up to 100 years, but—as said—it would require years of intense learning. The Chinese, after 2,500 years, have not stopped at face reading, but they also have developed complete analyses of what we can read from the human body, hands, eyes and the language of each of them.

Besides entertainment, is there any practical use for face reading? Yes, indeed! For instance, if it can give even a little advice on selecting a good, compatible spouse or any other partner, that has value. It does not matter if you are already in a permanent relationship; Physiognomy can still teach you enormously valuable things. After studying your partner's facial features, you will understand so much more about them. Matters that used to drive

Catherine Zeta-Jones

Gold is the strongest element in this face. All Gold people were born under the lucky stars. The eyebrows on this face are of a slightly angular shape, meaning its owner is a dramatic personality and fame comes through adventure or showmanship.

you crazy may turn into facts that you can easily understand. Maybe after all, he or she isn't such an unscrupulous person, perhaps all your jealousy has been in vain…or perhaps you really should start paying more attention to your guy or gal.

As we said on the starting pages of the book, you should read this publication with a mirror right next to you. Maybe the problem isn't always in the other person? That sounds impossible, you may think, but there is a chance that we, too, could be at fault! It is very important to remember that not all who have wrinkles at the outer corner of their eye are philanderers, or that not all people that have a big nose automatically become filthy rich. The wisdom of Physiognomy uses terms such as "may be" or "has a tendency to" or "a person like this sometimes…." Meaning that these are not rules, but possibilities. We are all individuals—luckily—and no rule that applies to one of us automatically applies to another. If your partner, friend or relative "is a person that may have a tendency to…" read the word "may" twice, and after that, continue observing and make your determination accordingly.

Help for Choosing a Career

If you are young, and you still have not decided what you wish to do in your life, Physiognomy may give you excellent pieces of advice. After all, why start to play the violin if all your features lean toward sports? Remember to use the mirror! If you already are fully engaged in your career but yearn to try something new, or if you have any friends, relatives or colleagues that are in a similar situation, start reading faces. It's no good to spend the rest of your life teaching mathematics to not-interested teenagers, when all you really want to do is to work, teach and perform in the arts!

Anthony Hopkins

The eyes are very soft, so this person is a kind and nurturing person. The face is heart shaped and it is a combination of Water and Wood. The owner of a face like this is very kind hearted. The nose tells that he enjoys making good business deals and he has the ability to enjoy them.

Sharon Stone

This beautiful face belongs to the Gold element, which is the perfect balance in face shapes. Even though we are talking about Chinese face reading, the ancient Greeks saw the perfect face to be similar to this. It is the oblong shape, and each third of the face is of equal length and about the same width, though narrower than it is wide. Gold people have grace and charm and they are fortunate and achieve high social standing.

Facelifts and Nose Jobs

Will a larger nose make me richer? Well, if you read everything in this book before this chapter, you almost know the answer. If you can afford a nose job, it might at first—because of the cost of the operation—make you less wealthy. It most certainly will not make you richer just because you changed to the larger size. But, you may think more highly of yourself and become more money-wise than ever before, and that may help you earn more money. Also, other people may think of you as a wealthier person and that may, repeat, may bring you more money. But as for Physiognomy, Chinese studies have found very little in common with getting rich and a nose that is larger due to a surgical operation; in most cases only the surgeon gets richer. This applies to all face-changing operations. In Chinese culture, wealth does not always mean a lot of money, but the word has also such meanings as good life, excellent health, large family, trustful friends, tasty food and drinks; all the good things in life. The bottom line is that in general, we cannot change our past, present or future by changing our facial features. An operation may change the way other people think of us, but the fact is that we have inherited most of our destiny with our genes, and in most cases only what we personally do may slightly alter that.

At the time of writing this book, one of our face reading clients was a wealthy businessman. He was in his late fifties, and worried about the three very visible horizontal lines on his forehead. It was his opinion that the lines that had grown deeper with the years made him look older and people would not respect him as much as before. After a detailed face reading and a long discussion about Physiognomy, the man realized the operation would serve no purpose. "Thank you," he said when leaving. "You saved me $20,000."

Even ugly faces are worth looking at—and that is a great comfort for most people.

Chinese proverb.

Woody Allen

A very interesting face. A typical triangular face, narrow at the bottom, widening to a broad forehead, and it belongs to the Wood element. Wood people are wise; so artists, scientists and thinkers are of this element. The nose is very strong and it is a very accumulative nose. The ears are very good and show that he has a kind disposition.

CHAPTER SIX: CLOSING

Health Care

The Chinese medicine and the Western medicine have a lot of differences. In the ancient Chinese studies, each section of the face has a referring section in the body. For instance, a gray or greenish color in the ears tells about medical problems in the kidneys; a yellowish or reddish color in the eye whites reveals that there's something wrong in the liver. The counterpart for the nose is the lungs, but for men it is the sexual organ. If the nose is too reddish or gray or greenish, or too pale, there are problems in either lungs or sexual organs. The woman's mouth represents the sexual organ and the spleen. For both sexes, the mouth should not be too moist or dry, not too colorless or dark.

Even though Western culture's way of thinking, especially its medicine, does not fully approve of the Chinese face reading claims, there are numerous facts that both sides agree on. Most importantly, when we see something wrong in a face that represents another area in that person's body, we should pay special attention to it. This could indicate a condition that requires medical attention, and the earlier we find what's wrong, the easier it is to cure. That does not mean that if your face looks perfect and your laugh lines are long and extend into the bottom zone, you should not pay any attention to your health. Our faces tell us a great deal about our potential gifts and possibilities. At the same time, humanity has numerous times shown how it can and will destroy almost everything that is extremely valuable to itself.

So, let's try to live wisely, and use the advantages that we have been given, and of which our face can tell!

Some people are wise,
and some are otherwise.

Mark Twain

ABOUT THE AUTHORS

Erik and Ilona Kanto have been married 27 years, and together have worked nearly three and a half decades in the arts and almost a quarter of a century in the media. Their achievements and contacts in the print and television media, especially in Hollywood, California, have made the impressive photo selection of this book possible. Peter Shen, a Physiognomy expert, did a face reading of Erik, and disclosed as the following:

Gold and Wood are the main elements in this face. With these features, the owner usually feels at home in society events and glamorous parties. Actors and artists are often Wood people; they are artistic, very creative and full of great ideas. Yet, when the face also has the Gold element mixed with Wood, it may create a conflict. Gold and Wood are not a good combination, as Gold hinders Wood. That is why the owner of a face like this, even though he has tons of great ideas, even though he really feels at home in the brightest lime lights, feels that he is not able to achieve nearly enough of his goals.

Long, well-formed ears tell about their owner's warm heart, the nose is evenly formed and there is some femininity around the mouth. A mole on the left cheek or chin is a so-called society mole and it notifies how much its owner enjoys being in the middle of everything. And that also means that he has all the possibilities to do that. Almost always this mole is on the left side of a man's face, but on the right side of a woman's face. Elizabeth Taylor is a good example of that.

Peter Shen said this of Ilona:

The face is mostly of the Water element combined with a large amount of Wood. If she were strictly Water, the face would be rounder. In general, this combination is very good, especially for a woman, because she is able to create a career outside the home at the same time as working as a housewife. The problem is that even though this person—in theory—has the capacity to do many things, in reality she expects so much from herself that it hinders and weakens the final result. Reading her face, we can easily see that the cheekbones are rather high, and that means that she has a lot of power. Compared to Erik's cheekbones, one would easily say she is the boss in the home. But please note: Softness on her high cheekbones conflicts with power, and brings the level of authority down.

The eyes are somewhat deep, meaning that she wants things run her way; also, the mouth, which is relatively small, hints of stubbornness. A lot of ideas are born under these facial features, and some may sometimes call her aggressive, in a controlled way.

As for Erik and Ilona as a married couple, according to Peter Shen's reading: Wood and Wood are not the best combination for a couple, because both keep creating ideas, and nobody goes ahead and fulfills them. On the other hand, their other elements, Gold and Water, go together very well, as Gold helps and supports Water. Those elements clearly aid each other, and together the end results can be fully successful.

MORE INFORMATION

More information is available at
www.facereading.cx

For additional questions, please send your mail to:

facereading.cx
P. O. Box 630402
Simi Valley, CA 93063-0402, USA

or send email to:
info@facereading.cx

Love is like measles.
You only get it once.
The older you are, the tougher it goes.

Howard Keel

INDEX

Erik Kanto is a Hollywood writer and the face-reading guru to the stars. Here's Erik chumming with superstar Uma Thurman, in one of this book's many celebrity photos.

FACE READING SHOW

Why not book a Face Reading Show and Lecture to your party, conference, or any other event?

Erik Kanto, an expert of the Chinese Art of Face Reading, has created a special 30 to 60-minute entertaining presentation where he teaches the audience the secrets of face reading. Using his own multimedia projector, the show is full of images of Hollywood celebrities and readings of their facial features.

Erik has entertained audiences all around the world, in all sizes of events from compact family get-togethers to large concert halls and cruises.

The Face Reading Show is excellent for holiday parties, to cheer up long conferences, conventions, birthdays, family reunions, etc., anywhere in the world!

For availability and further details, please contact Erik Kanto
by email: **erikkanto@facereading.cx**
by fax: **1-310-507-0142**
or by mail:

Erik Kanto
Kanto Productions LLC
P. O. Box 630402
Simi Valley, CA 93063-0402
USA

Please include your name, address, phone and email (if available).

Give This Book as a Gift

to a friend, colleague,
or member of your family!

Check your local bookstore or order directly from the authors.

- You may go to the website **www.facereading.cx**, order the book online and pay with your credit card.

- You may also order by regular mail and send:
  - Your name and full address
  - Phone number
  - Email address (if available)
  - Number of books ordered.
  - Check or money order made payable to Kanto Productions LLC

The price of YOUR FACE TELLS ALL is US$23.95 each, plus $4.00 shipping (in USA) for the first book, $2.00 for each additional book. California residents, please add $1.98 sales tax per book. Delivery time 2 - 6 weeks. Send your order to:

Kanto Productions LLC
Department 108
P. O. Box 630402
Simi Valley, CA 93063-0402

For orders outside the USA, please use the online ordering at www.facereading.cx.

Questions? info@facereading.cx or (800) 335-2686

ORDER A PERSONAL FACE READING

from the experts, the authors of this book!

You may order a detailed face reading for one person, or two persons in a partnership (marriage, business, etc.). A reading for two also compares the features that bond or separate those two persons.

Please send us:

- Two good photos **of the face**, one front, one side of the face. Photos may be black and white, but color is better. The size should be at least 3" x 4", the larger the better. Do not send original photos, as the material will not be returned.
- Name(s) of the person(s) in the photos, month and date of birth, as well as any other information you may think is important.
- Your name and full address
- Phone number and Email address (if available)
- Check or money order made payable to Kanto Productions LLC

The price of one personal, written face reading is US$59.00.Delivery by email as a printable PDF file(s) with your photo(s) is free worldwide. Delivery as a laser printed reading(s) with photo(s) in the USA by Priority Mail is $4.50, by FedEx $12.00. California residents, please add sales tax $4.87 per each face reading delivered to you printed. Faces are read in the order they arrive, usually in 2-6 weeks. Send your order to:

Kanto Productions LLC
Department 108
P. O. Box 630402
Simi Valley, CA 93063-0402

To see a sample of a typical face reading, or if you wish to order on the Internet and send photos via email, go to www.facereading.cx.

Questions?   info@facereading.cx   or   (800) 335-2686